25

D1108184

Prayers for Peace

ILLUSTRATED BY
RUTH McCREA

PETER PAUPER PRESS
MOUNT VERNON · NEW YORK

PRAYERS
FOR
PEACE

PRAYERS FOR PEACE

O GOD our Father, on this Day of Remembrance, look upon the unrest of the world and be pleased to complete the work of Thy healing hand. Send peace upon the earth, a deeper and more lasting peace than the world has ever known. Draw all men unto Thyself, and to one another by the bands of love. Grant understanding to the Nations with an increase of sympathy and mutual good will, that they may be united in a sacred Brotherhood wherein justice, mercy and faith, truth and freedom may flourish, so that the sacrifice of those who died may not have been made in vain.

A Chain of Prayers Across the Ages

I OFFER to Thee prayers for all those whom I have in any way grieved, vexed and oppressed, by word or deed, knowingly or unknowingly, that Thou mayest equally forgive us all our sins, and all our offenses against each other.

Take away, O Lord, from our hearts all suspiciousness, indignation, anger and contention, and whatever is likely to wound charity and to lessen brotherly love.

Have mercy, O Lord, have mercy on those who seek Thy mercy; give grace to the needy; make us so to live that we may be found worthy to enjoy the fruits of Thy grace.

Thomas à Kempis

PEACE I leave with you; my peace I give unto you. Not as the world giveth, give I unto you. Let not your heart be troubled, neither let it be afraid.

John 14:27

O GOD, make the door of this house wide enough
to receive all who need human love and fellowship, narrow enough to shut out all envy, pride
and strife.

Make its threshold smooth enough to be no
stumbling-block to children, nor to straying feet,
but rugged and strong enough to turn back the
tempter's power. God make the door of this house
the gateway to Thine eternal kingdom.

Door of St. Stephen's, London

ALMIGHTY God, Who hast created man in Thine
own image; grant us grace fearlessly to contend
against evil, and to make no peace with oppres-
sion; and, that we may reverently use our freedom, help us to employ it in the maintenance of
justice among men and nations, to the glory of
Thy Holy Name.

Prayers, New and Old

GRANT us peace, Thy most precious gift, O Thou eternal source of peace, and enable Israel to be its messenger unto the peoples of the earth. Bless our country that it may ever be a stronghold of peace, and its advocate in the council of nations. May contentment reign within its borders, health and happiness within its homes. Strengthen the bonds of friendship and fellowship among all inhabitants of our land. Plant virtue in every soul, and may the love of Thy name hallow every home and every heart. Praised be Thou, O Lord, Giver of Peace.

Adaptation of Ancient Hebrew Prayer,
First Century, B.C.

Ah! when shall all men's good
Be each man's rule, and universal Peace
Lie like a shaft of light across the land,
And like a lane of beams athwart the sea?

Alfred Lord Tennyson

THE PEACE of God which passeth all understanding, keep our hearts and minds in the knowledge and love of God, and of His Son Jesus Christ our Lord, and the blessing of God Almighty, the Father, the Son, and the Holy Ghost, be amongst you and remain with you always.

The Book of Common Prayer

LET ME not seek out of Thee what I can find only in Thee, O Lord, peace and rest and joy and bliss, which abide only in Thine abiding joy. Lift up my soul above the weary round or harassing thoughts to Thy eternal Presence. Lift up my soul to the pure, bright, serene, radiant atmosphere of Thy Presence, that there I may breathe freely, there repose in Thy love, there be at rest from myself, and from all things that weary me; and thence return, arrayed with Thy peace, to do and bear what shall please Thee. *E. B. Pusey*

O Thou who art Love, and who seest all the suffering, injustice and misery which reign in this world; look mercifully upon the poor, the oppressed, and all who are heavy laden with labor and sorrow. Fill our hearts with deep compassion for those who suffer, and hasten the coming of Thy kingdom of justice, truth and peace.

Source Unknown

Increase, O God, the spirit of neighborliness among us, that in peril we may uphold one another, in calamity serve one another, in suffering tend one another, and in homelessness, loneliness or exile befriend one another. Grant us brave and enduring hearts that we may strengthen one another, till the disciplines and testing of these days be ended, and Thou dost give again peace in our time.

Those who frequented the air-raid shelters in Hull, Birmingham and Westminster (England) made wide use of this prayer.

O LORD God everlasting, Which reignest over the kingdoms of men, so teach me I humbly beseech Thee, Thy word, and so strengthen me with Thy grace that I may feed Thy people with a faithful and a true heart, and rule them prudently with power. O Lord, Thou hast set me on high. My flesh is frail and weak. If I therefore at any time forget Thee, touch my heart, O Lord, that I may again remember Thee. If I swell against Thee, pluck me down in my own conceit.... I acknowledge, O my King, without Thee my throne is unstable, my seat unsure, my kingdom tottering, my life uncertain. I see all things in this life subject to mutability, nothing to continue still at one stay. Create therefore in me, O Lord, a new heart, and so renew my spirit that Thy law may be my study, Thy Truth, my delight, Thy church my care, Thy people my crown, Thy righteousness my pleasure, Thy service my government; so shall this my kingdom through Thee be established with peace.   *Queen Elizabeth I*

God of our fathers, known of old —
    Lord of our far-flung battle line —
Beneath whose awful hand we hold
    Dominion over palm and pine —
Lord God of Hosts, be with us yet,
Lest we forget — lest we forget!

The tumult and the shouting dies —
    The Captains and the Kings depart —
Still stands Thine ancient sacrifice,
    An humble and a contrite heart.
Lord God of Hosts, be with us yet,
Lest we forget — lest we forget!

Far-called, our navies melt away —
    On dune and headland sinks the fire —
Lo, all our pomp of yesterday
    Is one with Nineveh and Tyre!
Judge of the Nations, spare us yet,
Lest we forget — lest we forget!

If, drunk with sight of power, we loose

    Wild tongues that have not Thee in awe —

Such boasting as the Gentiles use,

    Or lesser breeds without the Law—

Lord God of Hosts, be with us yet,

Lest we forget — lest we forget!

For heathen heart that puts her trust

    In reeking tube and iron shard —

All valiant dust that builds on dust,

    And guarding calls not Thee to guard —

For frantic boast and foolish word,

Thy Mercy on Thy People, Lord!

                      Rudyard Kipling

Kipling sent the above poem to the London Times *with a letter, in which he said, "Enclosed please find my sentiments on things — which I hope are yours. We've been blowing up the Trumpets of the New Moon a little too much for white men, and it's about time we sobered down. If you like it, it's at your service — on the old conditions that I can use it if I want it later in book form. The sooner it's in print the better."*

The Recessional *was published in the London* Times. *The editor asked Kipling to name his own price for the poem, but the latter refused to accept any payment. The poem instantly sprang into world-wide popularity among English-speaking peoples.*

GRANT unto us, Almighty God, the peace of God that passeth understanding, that we, amid the storms and troubles of this our life, may rest in Thee, knowing that all things are in Thee; not beneath Thine eye only, but under Thy care, governed by Thy will, guarded by Thy love, so that with a quiet heart we may see the storms of life, the cloud and the thick darkness, ever rejoicing to know that the darkness and the light are both alike to Thee. Guide, guard, and govern us even to the end, that none of us may fail to lay hold upon the immortal life. *George Dawson*

O LORD, support us all the day long, until the shadows lengthen and the evening comes, and the busy world is hushed, and the fever of life is over, and our work is done. Then in thy mercy grant us a safe lodging, and a holy rest, and peace at the last. *Sixteenth Century*

ALMIGHTY God, who are the only source of health and healing, the spirit of calm and central peace of the universe: grant to us, Thy children, such a consciousness of Thy indwelling presence as may give us utter confidence in Thee. In all pain and weariness and anxiety may we throw ourselves upon Thy besetting care, that knowing ourselves fenced about by Thy loving omnipotence, we may permit Thee to give us health and strength and peace.

James Thayer Addison

O GOD, by Thy mercy strengthen us who lie exposed to the rough storms of troubles and temptations. Help us against our own negligence and cowardice, and defend us from the treachery of our unfaithful hearts. Succor us, we beseech Thee, and bring us to Thy safe haven of peace and felicity.

St. Augustine

O GOD of peace, we turn aside from an unquiet world, seeking rest for our spirits, and light for our thoughts. We bring our work to be sanctified, our wounds to be healed, our sins to be forgiven, our hopes to be renewed, our better selves to be quickened. O Thou, in whom there is harmony, draw us to thyself, and silence the discords of our wasteful lives. Thou in whom all are one, take us out of the loneliness of self, and fill us with the fullness of Thy truth and love. Thou whose greatness is beyond our highest praise, lift us above our common littleness and our daily imperfections; send us visions of the love that is in Thee and of the good that may be in us.

Source Unknown

GOD grant me the serenity to accept the things I cannot change, the courage to change the things I can, and the wisdom to distinguish the one from the other.

Reinhold Niebuhr

BLESSED is every one that feareth the Lord; that walketh in His ways. For thou shalt eat the labour of thine hands: happy shalt thou be, and it shall be well with thee. Thy wife shall be as a fruitful vine by the sides of thine house: thy children like olive plants round about thy table. Behold, that thus shall the man be blessed that feareth the Lord. The Lord shall bless thee out of Zion: and thou shalt see the good of Jerusalem all the days of thy life. Yea, thou shalt see thy children's children, and peace upon Israel.

Psalm CXXVIII

MAY THE blessings of the Lord rest upon all His people in every land, of every tongue. The Lord meet in mercy all that seek Him. The Lord comfort all that suffer and mourn. The Lord hasten His coming, and give us and all His people peace both now and forever more.

War-Time Prayers

LORD, make me an instrument of Thy peace. Where there is hatred, let me sow love; where there is doubt, faith; where there is despair, hope; where there is darkness, light; and where there is sadness, joy.

O Divine Master, grant that I may not so much seek to be consoled, as to console; to be understood, as to understand; to be loved, as to love; for it is in giving that we receive; it is in pardoning that we are pardoned, and it is in dying that we are born to eternal life.

Saint Francis of Assisi

O GOD, who tellest the number of the stars, and callest them all by their names; heal, we beseech Thee, the contrite in heart, and gather together the outcasts, and enrich us with the fullness of Thy wisdom and peace.

Sarum Breviary

MAY I be no man's enemy, and may I be the friend of that which is eternal and abides. May I never quarrel with those nearest me; and if I do, may I be reconciled quickly. May I never devise evil against any man; if any devise evil against me, may I escape uninjured and without the need of hurting him. May I love, seek, and attain only that which is good. May I wish for all men's happiness and envy none. May I never rejoice in the ill-fortune of one who has wronged me. When I have done or said what is wrong, may I never wait for the rebuke of others, but always rebuke myself until I make amends. . . . May I win no victory that harms either me or my opponent. . . . May I reconcile friends who are wroth with one another. May I, to the extent of my power, give all needful help to my friends and to all who are in want. May I never fail a friend in danger. When visiting those in grief may I be able by

gentle and healing words to soften their pain. . . .
May I respect myself. . . . May I always keep
tame that which rages within me. . . . May I
accustom myself to be gentle, and never be angry
with people because of circumstances. May I
never discuss who is wicked and what wicked
things he has done, but know good men and
follow in their footsteps. *Eusebius*

FORGIVE me, most gracious Lord and Father, if
this day I have done or said anything to increase
the pain of the world. Pardon the unkind word,
the impatient gesture, the hard and selfish deed,
the failure to show sympathy and kindly help
where I had the opportunity, but missed it; and
enable me so to live that I may daily do some-
thing to lessen the tide of human sorrow, and
add to the sum of human happiness.

F. B. Meyer

GRANT us peace, and establish Thy truth in us, as Thou fillest all things living with plenteousness. Remember every faithful soul in trial, and comfort, if it be possible, everyone in sorrow and distress. O Helper of the helpless, bring the wanderer home, and give health to the sick, and deliverance to the captive. Sustain the aged, comfort the weak-hearted, set free those whose souls are bound in misery and iron; remember all those who are in affliction, necessity, and emergency everywhere. Let us dwell with Thee in peace, as children of light, and in Thy light, Lord, let us see the light.

Direct, O Lord, in peace, the close of our life, trustfully, fearlessly, and, if it be Thy will, painlessly. Gather us when Thou wilt, into the abode of Thy chosen, without shame, or stain, or sin.

Rowland Williams

O LORD, the Author and Persuader of peace, love, and good-will, soften our hard and steely hearts, warm our icy and frozen hearts, that we may wish well to one another, and may be the true disciples of Jesus Christ. And give us grace even now to begin to show forth that heavenly life, wherein there is no disagreement nor hatred, but peace and love on all hands, one toward another. Amen.

Ludovicus Vives

O THOU full of compassion, I commit and commend myself unto Thee, in whom I am, and live, and know. Be Thou the Goal of my pilgrimage, and my Rest by the way. Let my soul take refuge from the crowding turmoil of worldly thoughts beneath the shadow of Thy wings; let my heart, this sea of restless waves, find peace in Thee, O God.

St. Augustine

LORD, though I am a miserable and wretched creature, I am in Covenant with Thee through grace. And I may, I will, come to Thee, for Thy People. Thou hast made me, though very unworthy, a mean instrument to do them some good, and Thee service; and many of them have set too high a value upon me, though others wish and would be glad of my death; Lord, however Thou dost dispose of me, continue and go on to do good for them. Give them consistency of judgment, one heart, and mutual love; and go on to deliver them, and with the work of reformation; and make the Name of Christ glorious in the world. Teach those who look too much on Thy instruments, to depend more upon Thyself. Pardon such as desire to trample upon the dust of a poor worm, for they are Thy People too. And pardon the folly of this short Prayer. And give us a good night, if it be Thy pleasure.

Oliver Cromwell

QUICKEN our consciences, O God, to feel the sin and shame of war. Inspire us with faith and courage to lift up our voices against private greed, social injustice, the aggression of the strong against the weak, and whatsoever else works enmity between man and man, class and class, nation and nation. Create within us a passion for the reign of righteousness, good will and brotherhood, and so fulfill Thine ancient word, "Nation shall not lift up sword against nation, neither shall they learn war any more."

War-Time Prayers

O GOD, who art Love, grant to Thy children to bear one another's burdens in perfect good will, that Thy peace which passeth understanding may keep our hearts and minds in Christ Jesus our Lord.

Source Unknown

PEACEFUL be earth, peaceful heaven, peaceful waters, peaceful trees. May all gods bring me peace. May there be peace through these invocations of peace. With these invocations of peace which appease everything, I render peaceful whatever here is terrible, whatever here is cruel, whatever here is sinful. Let it become auspicious, let everything be beneficial to us.

Hindu Prayer, Tenth Century B.C.

ALMIGHTY God, who changes not, amid the strifes of the world grant us Thy peace; in all its changefulness be Thou our stay; deliver us from its vanities, and enable us to find our chief good in Thee. Let all bitterness and wrath, and evil-speaking be put away from us; may we be kind-hearted, and learn to forgive one another, even as Thou hast forgiven us, through Jesus Christ our Lord. *Source Unknown*

O MOST high, Almighty, good Lord God, to Thee belong praise, glory, honor, and all blessing!

Praised be my Lord God for all His creatures, and especially for our brother the sun, who brings us the day and who brings us the light; fair is he and shines with a very great splendor: O Lord, he signifies to us Thee!

Praised be my Lord for our sister the moon, and for the stars, the which He has set clear and lovely in heaven.

Praised be my Lord for our brother the wind, and for air and cloud, calms and all weather, by the which Thou upholdest life in all creatures.

Praised be my Lord for our sister water, who is very serviceable unto us and humble and precious and clean.

Praised be my Lord for our brother fire, through whom Thou givest us light in the darkness; and he is bright and pleasant and very mighty and strong.

Praised be my Lord for our mother the earth, the which doth sustain us and keep us and bringeth forth divers fruits and flowers of many colors, and grass.

Praised be my Lord for all those who pardon one another for His love's sake, and who endure weakness and tribulation: blessed are they who peaceably shall endure, for Thou, O most Highest, shalt give them a crown.

Praised be my Lord for our sister the death of the body, from which no man escapeth. Woe to him who dieth in mortal sin! Blessed are they who are found walking by Thy most holy will, for the second death shall have no power to do them harm.

Praise ye and bless the Lord, and give thanks unto Him, and serve Him with great humility.

St. Francis of Assisi

O GOD, our help in ages past, our hope today and forever, have mercy upon humanity in its blindness, its bitterness, and its confusion. Deliver us, O Lord, from lust of power, from vanity of spirit, from envy, apathy, and ill-will. Touch our minds with light, that, having a right understanding, we may have compassion, and courage, and patience — working with Thy help for the better order of the ages.

Source Unknown

TEACH us, O Lord, to check in ourselves and in others every temper which makes for war, all ungenerous judgments, all promptings of self-assertion, all presumptuous claims; that being ever ready to recognize the needs and aspirations of other nations, we may, with patience, do whatsoever in us lies to remove suspicions and misunderstandings, and to honor all men.

War-Time Prayers

O God, the physician of men and nations, the restorer of the years that have been destroyed; look upon the distractions of the world, and be pleased to complete the work of Thy healing hand; draw all men unto Thee and one to another by the bands of Thy love; make Thy Church one, and fill it with Thy Spirit, that by Thy power it may unite the world in a sacred brotherhood of nations, wherein justice, mercy and faith, truth and freedom may flourish, and Thou mayest be ever glorified; through Jesus Christ our Lord.

Acts of Devotion

Prayer is the peace of our spirit, the stillness of our thoughts, the evenness of recollection, the seat of meditation, the rest of our cares, and the calm of our tempest; prayer is the issue of a quiet mind, of untroubled thoughts, it is the daughter of charity and the sister of meekness.

Jeremy Taylor

DISMAYED by the strife and jealousy which are bringing ruin to peoples and nations, we turn, O Jesus, to Thy most loving Heart as our only hope. O God of mercy, with tears we invoke Thee to end wars and the horror of war. O King of Peace, we humbly implore the peace for which we long.

From Thy Sacred Heart Thou didst shed forth over the world divine charity, so that discord might end and love alone might reign among men. During Thy life on earth, Thy Heart beat with tender compassion for the sorrows of men. In this day, when hate often dominates, may Thy divine Heart be once more moved to pity.

Inspire rulers and peoples with counsels of meekness. Heal the discords that tear nations asunder. Thou Who didst shed Thy precious blood that they might live as brothers, bring men together once more in loving harmony. To the cry of the Apostle Peter: "Save us, Lord, we perish," Thou didst answer words of mercy and didst still the raging waves. Deign now to hear our trustful prayers and give back to the world order and peace.

And do thou, O most Holy Virgin, as in other times of distress, be our help, our protection, and our safeguard. *Benedict XV*

O God, our Ruler, give to every State a deeper sense of human brotherhood, a new respect for man and reverence for woman, new loyalty in service, compunction and charity, new happiness in work and justice in reward; that our homes may be restored in Thee, our cities rebuilt, and all the world may reflect the radiance of the Throne which is eternal in the heavens.

Source Unknown

GRACIOUS Lord, Thou art not the God of confusion or discord, but the God of concord and of peace; unite our hearts and affections in such sort together, that we may as brethren walk in Thy house, in brotherly charity and love, and as members of the body of Christ. Let the oil of sanctification that is Thy Holy Spirit inflame us, and the dew of Thy blessing continually fall upon us, that we may obtain life eternal.

From Scottish Psalter, Sixteenth Century A.D.

O THOU who art Love, and who seest all the suffering, injustice and misery which reign in this world; look mercifully upon the poor, the oppressed, and all who are heavy laden with labor and sorrow. Fill our hearts with deep compassion for those who suffer, help us to help them in the hour of their extremity, and hasten the coming of Thy blessed kingdom of justice and peace.

Source Unknown

GRANT, O Lord, that we may approach every question of foreign policy from the viewpoint of our Christian faith; that we may check in ourselves and in others every temper which makes for war, all ungenerous judgments, all presumptuous claims, all promptings of self-assertion, the growths of ignorance and passion; that we may endeavor to understand the needs, the feelings, the endowments, the traditional aspirations of other countries; that we may do gladly, unweariedly, patiently, what lies in us to remove suspicions and misunderstandings; that we may honor all men. Amen.

Bishop Brooke F. Westcott

ALMIGHTY God, in whose sight all of the creatures are equal, draw together all of the nations in friendship so that brother will be disposed to help his brother, and none of Thy people will live in want or in hunger.   *Source Unknown*

ALMIGHTY God, who hast given us this good land for our heritage; we humbly beseech Thee that we may always prove ourselves a people mindful of Thy favor and glad to do Thy will. Bless our land with honorable industry, sound learning, and pure manners. Save us from violence, discord, and confusion; from pride and arrogancy, and from every evil way. Defend our liberties, and fashion into one united people the multitudes brought hither out of many kindreds and tongues. Endue with the spirit of wisdom those to whom in Thy Name we entrust the authority of government, that there may be justice and peace at home, and that, through obedience to Thy law, we may show forth Thy praise among the nations of the earth. In the time of prosperity, fill our hearts with thankfulness, and in the day of trouble, suffer not our trust in Thee to fail. *The Book of Common Prayer*

PRAY not! The darkness will not brighter be!
Nought ask the silence, for it cannot speak!
Nought from the helpless gods by gift and hymn,
Within yourselves deliverance must be sought.
Nor bribe with blood, nor feed with fruit and
cakes.

Japanese (Buddhist), First Century B.C.

ALMIGHTY God, grant unto us, we beseech Thee, a succession of rulers learned in the wisdom of the kingdom of Christ. Endue our law-givers with a right understanding and a pure purpose; enable them to rise above all self-seeking and party zeal into the larger desire for public good and human brotherhood. Purge our public life of evil, subdue in the nation all thirst for conquest and vain-glory, and inspire us with calmness and self-restraint, to Thy honor and glory, Who ever liveth and reigneth, one God world without end.

Source Unknown

O Thou, who by Mind everlasting rulest the world, Maker of lands and sky, who orderest Time to flow from the beginning, and, Thyself at rest, makest all things move; whom no external causes urge to fashion the work of fluctuating matter, but the innate Form of the Highest Good, beyond all rivalry. Thou deducest all from a heavenly pattern, Thyself most beautiful, guiding a beautiful universe by Mind, moulding it to that Image, and commanding its perfect parts to combine for the perfection of the whole. Thou bindest the elements by numbers, that Cold should match with Heat, and Dry with Moist, lest the purer flame should fly off, or the heavy things overlay all lands. . . .

Grant, O Father, to our minds, to climb to that august abode, grant us to visit the Fountain of the Good, grant that, finding the Light, we may open wide and fix on Thee the eyes of our souls.

Scatter the mists and the heaviness of the earthly mass, and shine out with Thy own splendor: for Thou art the Serene, Thou the tranquil resting place of the pious: to behold Thee, is the aim. Thou art at once the beginning, the carrier, the guide, the pathway and the end.

Boethius

HEAVENLY Father, in whom is no darkness at all, nor any shadow that is cast by turning, forgive our feverish ways — our anxieties, our fears, our uncertainties. We are like children walking wilfully and blindly in darkness while the world without is ablaze with light. Open our eyes that we may see Thee; and our minds that we may understand and know Thee. Help us to make the great adventure of faith, and discover the secret of peace, in finding Thee, Thou great Companion of our souls.

Prayers for Faith and Trust

LORD, preserve Thy people; maintain true righteous justice and worldly government everywhere; so that all things may take place in an orderly way and peace may not be destroyed by revolution or secret enmity and plotting, nor the external good order be corrupted by debased and impure living or disturbed by other offenses. Amen.

Martin Luther, Sixteenth Century A.D.

O GOD, from whom all holy desires, all good counsels, and all just works do proceed; give unto Thy servants that peace which the world cannot give; that our hearts may be set to obey Thy commandments, and also that by Thee, we, being defended from the fear of our enemies, may pass our time in rest and quietness.

The Book of Common Prayer

O God, who art Peace everlasting, whose chosen reward is the gift of peace, and who hast taught us that the peacemakers are Thy children, pour Thy peace into our souls, that everything discordant may utterly vanish, and all that makes for peace be sweet to us forever. Amen.

O most merciful God, who are both the Mind of Thy creation and the Father of us all, send Thy light to Thy children who grope in mental darkness and the dimness of uncertain sight. Turn the night of their distress into the morning of Thy hope, and cause them and those who watch and wait to rest confidently in Peace. Amen.

In Thee, O Lord God, I place my whole hope and refuge; on Thee I rest all my tribulation and anguish; for I find all to be weak and inconstant, whatsoever I behold out of Thee. For many friends cannot profit, nor strong helpers assist, nor the books of the learned afford comfort, nor any place, however retired and lonely, give shelter, unless Thou Thyself dost assist, strengthen, console, instruct, and guard us. For all things that seem to belong to the attainment of peace and felicity, without Thee, are nothing, and do bring in truth no felicity at all. Thou therefore art the Fountain of all that is good; and to hope in Thee above all things is the strongest comfort of Thy servants. To Thee, therefore, do I lift up mine eyes; in Thee, my God, the Father of mercies, do I put my trust. Amen.   *Thomas à Kempis*

O GOD, who art the author of peace and lover of concord, in knowledge of whom standeth our eternal life, whose service is perfect freedom; defend us Thy humble servants in all assaults of our enemies; that we, surely trusting in Thy defense, may not fear the power of any adversaries.

The Book of Common Prayer

Lord, Thou hast been favorable unto Thy land: Thou hast brought back the captivity of Jacob. Thou hast forgiven the iniquity of Thy people; Thou hast covered all their sin. Selah. Thou hast taken away all Thy wrath: Thou hast turned Thyself from the fierceness of Thine anger. Turn us, O God of our salvation, and cause Thine anger toward us to cease. Wilt Thou be angry with us for ever? wilt Thou draw out Thine anger to all generations? Wilt Thou not revive us again: that Thy people may rejoice in Thee? Show us Thy mercy, O Lord, and grant us Thy salvation. I will hear what God the Lord will speak: for He will speak peace unto His people, and to His saints: but let them not turn again to folly. Surely His salvation is nigh them that fear Him; that glory may dwell in our land. Mercy and truth are met together; righteousness and peace have kissed each other. Truth shall spring out of the earth;

and righteousness shall look down from heaven. Yea, the Lord shall give that which is good; and our land shall yield her increase. Righteousness shall go before Him; and shall set us in the way of His steps.   *Psalm LXXXV*

GOD be merciful unto us, and bless us; and cause His face to shine upon us; Selah. That Thy way may be known upon earth, Thy saving health among all nations. Let the people praise Thee, O God; let all the people praise Thee. O let the nations be glad and sing for joy: for Thou shalt judge the people righteously, and govern the nations upon earth. Selah. Let the people praise Thee, O God; let all the people praise Thee. Then shall the earth yield her increase; and God, even our own God, shall bless us. God shall bless us; and all the ends of the earth shall fear Him.

Psalm LXVII

UNTO Thee will I cry, O Lord my rock; be not silent to me: lest if Thou be silent to me, I become like them that go down into the pit. Hear the voice of my supplications, when I cry unto Thee, when I lift up my hands toward Thy holy oracle. Draw me not away with the wicked, and with the workers of iniquity, which speak peace to their neighbors, but mischief is in their hearts. Give them according to their deeds, and according to the wickedness of their endeavors: give them after the work of their hands; render to them their desert. Because they regard not the work of the Lord, nor the operation of His hands, He shall destroy them, and not build them up. Blessed be the Lord, because He hath heard the voice of my supplications. The Lord is my strength and my shield; my heart trusted in Him, and I am helped: therefore my heart greatly rejoiceth; and with my song will I praise Him.

The Lord is their strength, and He is the saving strength of His anointed. Save Thy people, and bless Thine inheritance: feed them also, and lift them up for ever.

Psalm XXVIII

O LORD God Almighty, Thou art our Father, we are Thy children; Thou art our Redeemer, we Thy people, purchased with the price of Thy most precious blood: be pleased to moderate Thy anger towards Thy servants; let not Thy whole displeasure arise, lest we be consumed and brought to nothing. Let health and peace be within our dwellings; let righteousness and holiness dwell for ever in our hearts, and be expressed in all our actions, and the light of Thy countenance be upon us in all our sufferings, that we may delight in the service and in the mercies of God for ever. Amen.

Holy Living

HE WHO excels as a soldier is the one who is not warlike; he who fights the best fight is not wrathful; he who best conquers an enemy is not quarrelsome; he who best employs people is obedient himself. This is the virtue of not-quarreling, this is the secret of bringing out other men's ability, this is complying with heaven.

Lao Tzu, Sixth Century, B.C.

WITH malice toward none; with charity for all; with firmness in the right, as God gives us to see the right, let us strive on to finish the work we are in; to bind up the nation's wounds; to care for him who shall have borne the battle, and for his widow and his orphan — to do all which may achieve and cherish a just and lasting peace among ourselves and with all nations.

Abraham Lincoln

GOD is our refuge and strength, a very present help in trouble. Therefore will not we fear, though the earth be removed, and though the mountains be carried into the midst of the sea; though the waters thereof roar and be troubled, though the mountains shake with the swelling thereof. Selah. There is a river, the streams whereof shall make glad the city of God, the holy place of the tabernacles of the Most High. God is in the midst of her; she shall not be moved: God shall help her, and that right early. The heathen raged, the kingdoms were moved: He uttered His voice, the earth melted. The Lord of hosts is with us; the God of Jacob is our refuge. Selah. Come, behold the works of the Lord, what desolations He hath made in the earth. He maketh wars to cease unto the end of the earth; He breaketh the bow, and cutteth the spear in sunder; He burneth the chariot in the fire. Be still, and know that I am

God: I will be exalted among the heathen, I will be exalted in the earth. The Lord of hosts is with us; the God of Jacob is our refuge. Selah.

Psalm XLVI

I WAS glad when they said unto me, Let us go into the house of the Lord. Our feet shall stand within thy gates, O Jerusalem. Jerusalem is builded as a city that is compact together: whither the tribes go up, the tribes of the Lord, unto the testimony of Israel, to give thanks unto the name of the Lord. For there are set thrones of judgment, the thrones of the house of David. Pray for the peace of Jerusalem: they shall prosper that love Thee. Peace be within Thy walls, and prosperity within Thy palaces. For my brethren and companions' sakes, I will now say, Peace be within Thee. Because of the house of the Lord our God I will seek Thy good. *Psalm CXXII*

LORD, how are they increased that trouble me! many are they that rise up against me. Many there be which say of my soul, There is no help for him in God. Selah. But Thou, O Lord, art a shield for me; my glory, and the lifter up of mine head. I cried unto the Lord with my voice, and He heard me out of His holy hill. Selah. I laid me down and slept; I awaked; for the Lord sustained me. I will not be afraid of ten thousands of people, that have set themselves against me round about. Arise, O Lord; save me, O my God: for Thou hast smitten all mine enemies upon the cheek bone; Thou hast broken the teeth of the ungodly. Salvation belongeth unto the Lord: Thy blessing is upon Thy people. Selah.

Psalm III

BLESSED is the peace-maker, not the conqueror.

Ancient Proverb

How BEAUTIFUL upon the mountains are the feet of him that bringeth good tidings, that publisheth peace; that bringeth good tidings of good, that publisheth salvation; that saith unto Zion, Thy God reigneth! Thy watchmen shall lift up the voice; with the voice together shall they sing: for they shall see eye to eye, when the Lord shall bring again Zion. Break forth into joy, sing together, ye waste places of Jerusalem: for the Lord hath comforted His people, He hath redeemed Jerusalem. The Lord hath made bare His holy arm in the eye of all the nations; and all the ends of the earth shall see the salvation of our God.

Isaiah 7:7

PEACE, peace is what I seek, and public calm;
Endless extinction of unhappy hates.

Matthew Arnold

IN THE Lord put I my trust: how say ye to my soul, Flee as a bird to your mountain? For, lo, the wicked bend their bow, they make ready their arrow upon the string, that they may privily shoot at the upright in heart. If the foundations be destroyed, what can the righteous do? The Lord is in His holy temple, the Lord's throne is in heaven: His eyes behold, His eyelids try, the children of men. The Lord trieth the righteous: but the wicked and him that loveth violence his soul hateth. Upon the wicked He shall rain snares, fire and brimstone, and an horrible tempest this shall be the portion of their cup. For the righteous Lord loveth righteousness; his countenance doth behold the upright.   *Psalm XI*

GRANT, O Lord, that we may live in Thy fear, die in Thy favor, rest in Thy peace, rise in Thy power, reign in Thy glory.   *Archbishop Laud*

For lo! the days are hastening on,

 By prophet-bards foretold,

When with the ever-circling years,

 Comes round the age of gold;

When Peace shall over all the earth

 Its ancient splendors fling

And the whole world send back the song

 Which now the angels sing.

Edmund Hamilton Sears

Lord, behold our family here assembled. We thank Thee for this place in which we dwell; for the love that unites us; for the peace accorded us this day; for the hope with which we expect the morrow; for the health, the work, the food and the bright skies that make our lives delightful; for our friends in all parts of the earth, and our friendly helpers in this foreign isle.

Robert Louis Stevenson

UNTO God's gracious mercy and protection we commit ourselves. The Lord bless us and keep us. The Lord make His face to shine upon us and be gracious unto us. The Lord lift up the light of His countenance upon us, and give us peace, both now and evermore.

Numbers 6:24-26

THEY shall beat their swords into plowshares, and their spears into pruning hooks; nation shall not lift up sword against nation, neither shall they learn war any more.

Isaiah, ii, 2-4

P E A C E